P9-DNE-737

Marc Chagall in 1910

I am Marc Chagall.

You might be wondering why I painted flying goats and fish, green-faced fiddlers perched on roofs, houses in the sky floating upside down, lovers flying effortlessly over the city.

I painted my world, my life, all the things I loved, all the things I dreamed of, all the things I could not say in words. I painted my beloved Russia, my hometown, Vitebsk, the Jewish neighborhood where I grew up, the way I saw everything as a child.

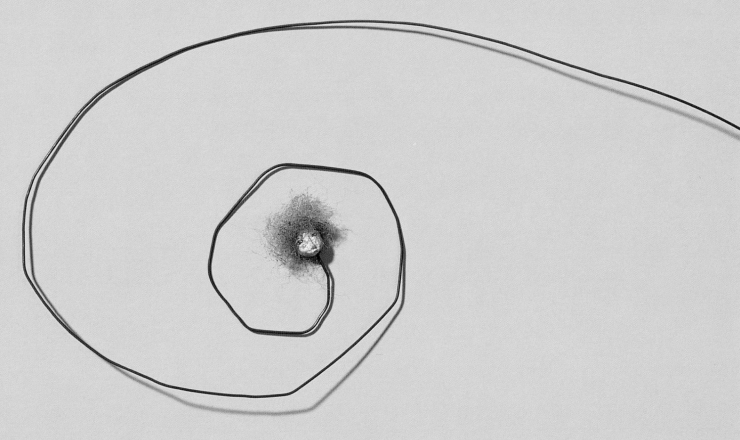

To my parents, who gave me free reign to pursue my dreams,
and to my brother, with boundless love

My special thanks to the Center of Hebrew Contemporary Documentation Foundation
in Milan and to Nanette R. Hayon Zippel for her kindness
— B. L.

Photograph of Marc Chagall, 1910, on concession from the Ida Chagall Paris Archives
Photographs of Bimba Landmann's artwork © Allessandro Vicario
© Edizioni Arka, Milan, Italy 2005

This edition published 2006 in the United States of America by
Eerdmans Books for Young Readers
An imprint of Wm. B. Eerdmans Publishing Company
255 Jefferson SE, Grand Rapids, Michigan 49503
P.O. Box 163, Cambridge CB3 9PU U.K.
www.eerdmans.com/youngreaders

ISBN 0-8028-5305-6

06 07 08 09 10   6 5 4 3 2 1

Printed in Italy

A catalog record of this book is available from the Library of Congress.
Matthew Van Zomeren, Graphic Designer

I Am
Marc Chagall

Text and illustrations by Bimba Landmann
Text loosely inspired by *My Life* by Marc Chagall

Eerdmans Books for Young Readers
Grand Rapids, Michigan • Cambridge, U.K.

I grew up in Vitebsk, a small Russian farming town.

I loved its goats and hens and cows, its small wooden houses, its men with violins, their songs and prayers, its lights of Shabbat, the Jewish Sabbath, the candles in the windows.

At night the sky would echo with hymns, "*Shalom Aleikhem*. Peace unto you." And angels would follow the head of each family home from the synagogue.

Then the feast would begin: noodles, stuffed fish, meat with carrots, stewed fruit. After the last prayers were said, while my family dozed off, I would go sit on the roof. I loved it up there with the moon and my stars.

There I would dream about what I might become. Not a butcher, like my grandfather. Not a barber, like Uncle Zoussy. Certainly not a shop assistant, like my father, who hauled around heavy barrels of brine-soaked herring every day. No, I dreamed of a bright future, of becoming perhaps a famous musician, or a dancer, or a poet.

These dreams made me happy, like I was flying over Vitebsk, over all of Russia.

My parents, however, had different plans for me. They sent me to a school in the rabbi's house where the Jewish religion was taught. There I had to learn Hebrew and study the Torah, the sacred book, and listen to the rabbi's teachings.

Often, however, I was distracted. Instead of listening, I watched the baby in its cradle, the goat sticking its head through the window, the hens pecking at the floor.

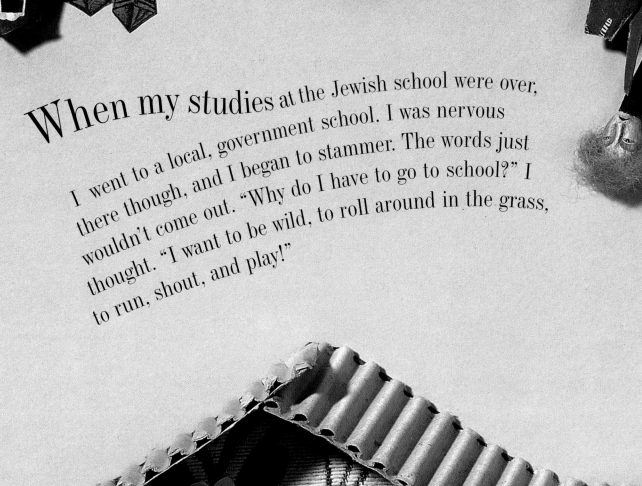

When my studies at the Jewish school were over, I went to a local, government school. I was nervous there though, and I began to stammer. The words just wouldn't come out. "Why do I have to go to school?" I thought. "I want to be wild, to roll around in the grass, to run, shout, and play!"

The only lessons I liked were geometry and art,
where there was no need to talk — the lines and angles
and colors said everything. I was good at drawing, and
a friend said to me, "You must be a real artist." That
word seemed magical. An artist? Me?

I begged my mother to let me study art. "What?" she said. "For a Jew to want to be an artist is unheard of!" Finally she took me to an art teacher to ask his opinion. The teacher looked at my drawings in silence, thinking. Then he said I had some talent.

ШКОЛА ЖИВОПИСИ
И ХУДОЖНИКА
Г. ПЕН

That was all I needed to hear. I thought,
"Painting is as necessary as bread. It is my
window so I can fly to another world."

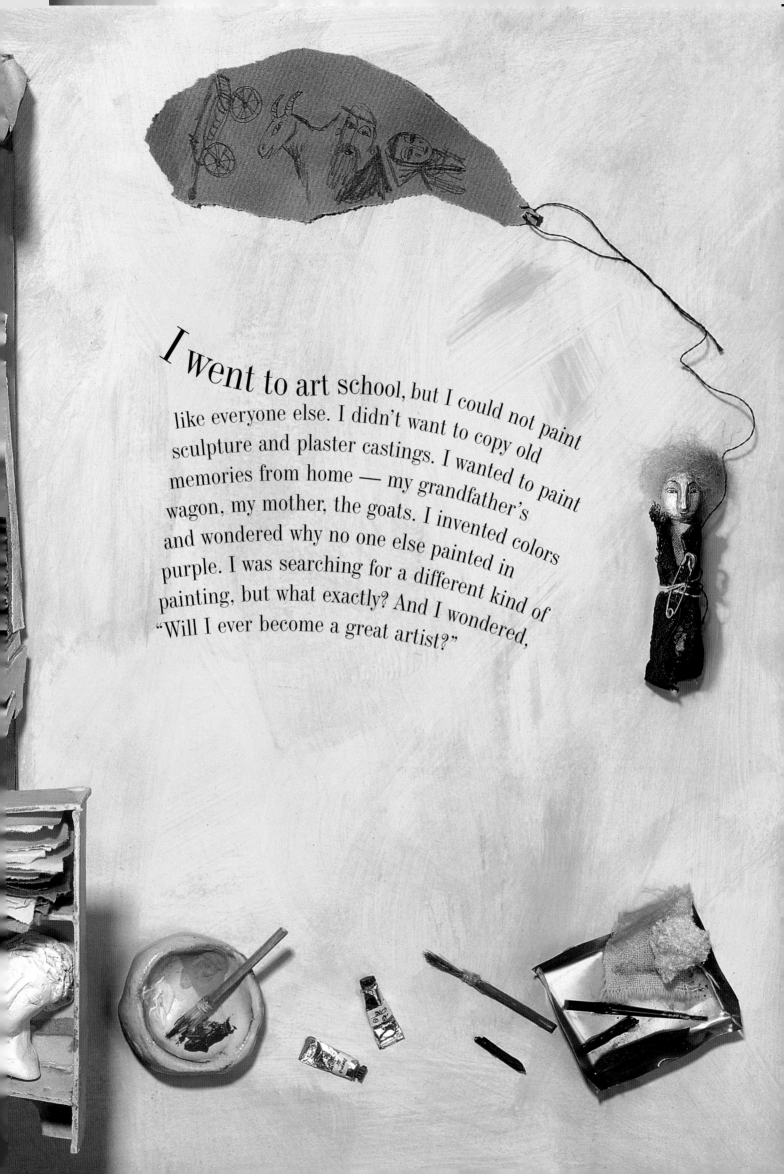

I went to art school, but I could not paint like everyone else. I didn't want to copy old sculpture and plaster castings. I wanted to paint memories from home — my grandfather's wagon, my mother, the goats. I invented colors and wondered why no one else painted in purple. I was searching for a different kind of painting, but what exactly? And I wondered, "Will I ever become a great artist?"

No one at home cared about my painting. My

father said, "Go find a proper job." So for a while I worked for a photographer, but I couldn't stop thinking about painting.

I went to a new art school in Saint Petersburg with only twenty-seven rubles in my pocket. I had to share a rented room. I even had to share my bed. I was starving and miserable, but my dream of painting kept me going.

Then one day I was arrested for not having a work permit. In jail, though, I lived well — I had a bed to myself, food to eat, and a place to draw in peace!

After two weeks in jail, my life continued

the same as before: a job here and there, painting school, cold uncomfortable nights. Every now and then I would return to Vitebsk for the holidays. There waiting for me was my own room where I could paint all day and all night long.

And Bella was there. Bella, my sweet girlfriend. She brought me cakes and fish and flowers and filled my room with love. She floated over my canvases for a long time and called me her twinkling star. I painted her all the time.

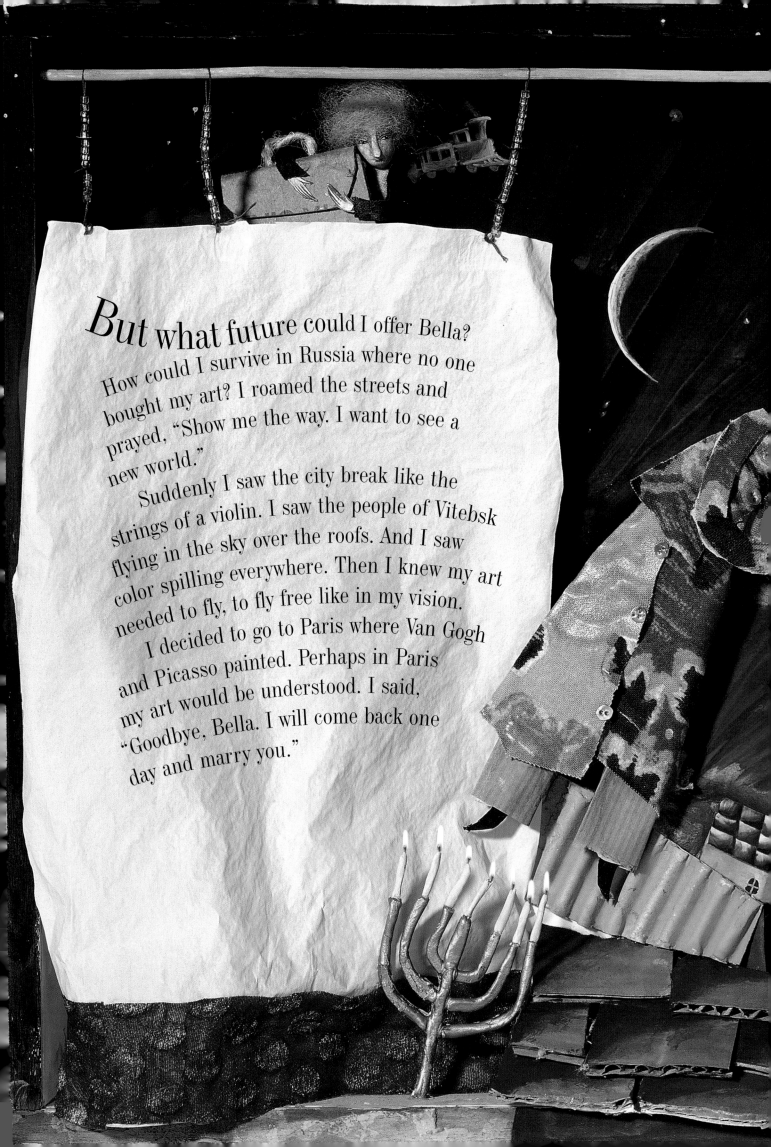

But what future could I offer Bella? How could I survive in Russia where no one bought my art? I roamed the streets and prayed, "Show me the way. I want to see a new world."

Suddenly I saw the city break like the strings of a violin. I saw the people of Vitebsk flying in the sky over the roofs. And I saw color spilling everywhere. Then I knew my art needed to fly, to fly free like in my vision.

I decided to go to Paris where Van Gogh and Picasso painted. Perhaps in Paris my art would be understood. I said, "Goodbye, Bella. I will come back one day and marry you."

Paris. What a city for a painter! Many

artists lived there, artists from all over the world.
I could hear sculptors chiseling away at their marble,
musicians strumming their guitars. Other painters,
like Modigliani, invited me to see their work. And
the poet Apollinaire came to see me. He read his
poems to me and said, "How odd and beautiful your
paintings are."

Did he say that because I didn't use perspective,
because I turned my canvases upside down, because I
painted on bits of tablecloths and sheets and shirts? Or
was it my improbable colors, my flying goats and cows?

I began to write poetry because it was as natural
as breathing. The Paris poets liked my work and called
me a poet-painter.

To me Paris was light, color, freedom, the sun, the joy of living. I painted there as if I were dreaming, and I always painted Vitebsk. I painted the colors of my memories and suddenly a peasant, a fiddler, Bella, or snow-covered wooden houses would appear. My entire family, the whole of Vitebsk, lived inside my paintings. I'd say to them in my mind, "Your lives and actions have become my art."

A friend helped me take my paintings of Vitebsk to an exhibition. He paraded them through the streets of Paris on a simple handcart!

At the exhibition many visitors saw my paintings.

There was always someone who would stand in front of my paintings and ask, "Why doesn't he paint like the rest? Why does he make a huge donkey and paint him green?"

But many of the visitors liked my paintings for what they were. In 1914 someone even took my paintings to Berlin for my first one-person show. There I finally began to make a name for myself.

Something troubled me though. I looked at other painters' work and saw colors of gloom and foreboding, like something bad was about to happen. When I traveled through Germany by train, going back to Vitebsk to see Bella and my family, I saw the reality with my own eyes — Europe was getting ready for war.

The war came to Russia like a cold, biting wind. I began to draw soldiers, the wounded on stretchers, men and women with sad faces. But I also painted Bella, our wedding, our little daughter, Ida.

After three long years of war, the Russian Revolution turned my country all upside down — like one of my paintings. To celebrate the first year of the Revolution, I was asked to make posters. Soon my brightly colored animals were paraded all over the city. I looked at the smiling faces of the children and workers and was sure they understood my art.

But the Russian leaders did not understand me. They asked more questions: "Why is the horse flying in the sky? Why is the cow green? What does this have to do with Russian politics?" I let them grumble and went to Moscow with Bella and Ida to paint a new Jewish theater. "Here are the blank walls," said the director. "Do whatever you want with them."

For forty days I worked until the walls, curtain, and ceiling were covered with paintings — a musician, a clown, a dancer, a dreaming poet, and all the peasants of my Vitebsk, including Bella, Ida, and myself.

In Moscow I also taught orphans of war. These children who had seen their world collapse took the colors and created drawings of fantasy and poetry. I was delighted to see that they understood that the world inside us is at times more real than the world outside.

I enjoyed teaching, but when it was time to be paid I was always told, "Come back tomorrow . . ." Once again I had no money.

Then a friend in Germany wrote to tell me that my paintings were selling well there. So we moved to Germany.

Next, a friend in France wrote and said, "You are famous here." So we moved again, this time to Paris. There I began to paint pictures from the Bible. I painted angels, and the story of Jacob who slept on a stone, and of David, the musician-king. I also painted light and flowers and was happy in Paris with Bella for many years — but not forever.

The Second World War broke out in Europe in 1941, so we took a ship to America. During the journey I wondered if the silent stars above could already see my future: my life in America; my return to France after the war; the museum of my paintings in Nice; my stained glass in Jerusalem, Chicago, New York; my mosaics . . .

Yes, perhaps the stars could already see my entire life traced out on the earth like a picture by Marc Chagall.

The Life of Marc Chagall

1887   Marc Chagall is born in Vitebsk, Russia.

1907   At age 19, he moves to Saint Petersburg to look for a job and enter art school.

1910   At 23, he goes to Paris to seek his fortune as an artist.

1914   He has his first one-person show in Berlin. He returns to Russia for a vacation, but the First World War breaks out, forcing him to stay in Vitebsk.

1915   He marries Bella Rosenfeld, and together they move to Saint Petersburg.

1916   Their daughter, Ida, is born.

1918   Chagall is appointed Commissar for the Fine Arts in Vitebsk, where he then lives. A year later he opens a school of painting.

1920   He moves to Moscow, where he paints for the Jewish Theater.

1922   He returns to Berlin with his family, where he begins illustrating his autobiography, *My Life*.

1923   He moves to Paris, where he is given many important commissions, one of which is producing engravings for the Bible.

1931   He and Bella travel to Palestine, where he draws inspiration for the stories from the Old Testament.

1933   In Basel, Switzerland, an important exhibition is organized in his honor. In Germany some of his paintings are burned because he is Jewish.

1941   After numerous trips around Europe, the outbreak of the Second World War forces Chagall to move first to Paris and then to flee to America. In America, Chagall creates scenes and costumes for Tchaikovsky and Stravinsky ballets.

1944   Bella dies, and Chagall stops painting for an entire year. Important exhibits of his work are organized at the Museum of Modern Art in New York, at the Museum of Modern Art in Paris, and at the Stedelijk Museum in Amsterdam.

1948   Chagall returns to France and settles in Vence, where he meets Vava Brodsky, whom he later marries when he is 65.

1957   He starts working on the art of stained glass in the Church of Assy in France.

1963   He paints the ceiling of the *Opera* in Paris.

1969   Chagall has a museum built in Nice to host his works. He produces several stained glass windows in Reims, Metz, Jerusalem, Zurich, New York, Chicago, and Nice, as well as mosaics and ceramics.

1973   Chagall returns to Russia, to Moscow and Leningrad (Saint Petersburg), invited by the Minister of Culture, but he doesn't go to Vitebsk. He'd rather remember his village the way it used to be.

1985   Chagall dies in his home in Vence when he is almost 98 years old.